Written by Neil Morris

Cartoons by Mark Davis

Miles Kelly
PUBLISHING

Projects created by
Ting Morris

Art direction
Clare Sleven

Design
Mackerel Design

Project management
Mark Darling

Artwork commissioned by
Lynne French, Susanne Grant, Natasha Smith

Art reference
Lesley Cartlidge, Liberty Mella

Editorial director
Paula Borton

First published in 2000 by
Miles Kelly Publishing Ltd
Bardfield Centre, Great Bardfield, Essex CM7 4SL

24681097531

British Library Cataloguing-in-Publication Data
A catalogue record for this book is available from the British Library

ISBN 1-90294-738-X

Printed in Hong Kong

Acknowledgements

The publishers wish to thank the following artists who have contributed to
this book:
Kuo Kang Chen, Rob Jakeway, Janos Marffy

The publishers wish to thank the following sources for the photographs
used in this book:
Genesis photo library: Page 22 (BL)
All other photographs from Miles Kelly Archives.

CONTENTS

PLANET EARTH

ocean

NEARLY THREE QUARTERS OF THE EARTH IS COVERED WITH OCEANS.

Our home, Earth, is a round planet that travels around the Sun in a part of the Universe called the Milky Way. A blanket of air is wrapped around the Earth, and this atmosphere allows humans, animals and plants to breathe and live. Looked at from space, our planet looks blue and white. The blue comes from the water which covers much of the Earth's surface, and the white patches are masses of clouds.

Earth has many special features, such as forests, mountains, deserts and oceans.

Factfile

- Earth's diameter is 12,756 km.
- Earth's circumference at the equator is 40,074 km.
- The Sahara is the biggest desert, stretching over 5,000 km from the Atlantic Ocean to the Red Sea.
- The Pacific is the biggest and deepest ocean; it covers more than a third of the Earth's surface.

mountains

- The highest mountain range is the Himalayas, in Asia; the longest is the Andes, in South America.

forest

desert

Earth on your window

1. Copy our blue and white planet Earth on your window. Powder paint mixed with water and washing-up liquid gives the most intense colours.

2. Paint on the inside of the window, so the rain can't ruin your artwork.

3. Tape newspaper to the bottom of the window to protect the window sill and floor.

4. You can wash the Earth off with a sponge and soapy water when you've grown tired of it or want to change planets.

MOON

Planet Earth has a satellite which circles around it as it travels through space. Satellites such as this are called moons, and we call ours simply the Moon. It is about a quarter the size of Earth, but it has no water and no air. Because it has no atmosphere and no weather, the Moon also has no life and it hardly changes. Its surface is covered with rocks and dust, as well as circular hollows called craters.

From Earth, the Moon appears to change shape because we see different parts of it lit by sunlight.

The Moon's diameter is just over a quarter the size of its mother planet, Earth.

new Moon

Factfile

- The Moon is 384,000 km from Earth; you would have to go around the Earth 9.5 times to travel this far.

- The Moon spins as it circles the Earth, so the same side always faces us.

- There are 29.5 days from one new Moon to the next.

- The Moon's craters were formed by chunks of space rock crashing into it.

WHAT'S ALL THIS ABOUT A 'SEA OF TRANQUILITY'?

Sea

Make a Moon calendar

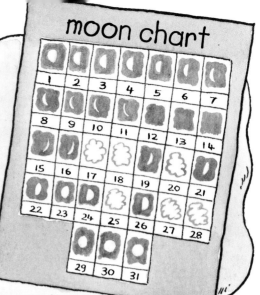

moon chart

1. Divide a large sheet of paper up into squares for the days of the month.

2. Each night, draw the shape of the Moon as you see it from your window. If the weather is clear, this will be easy. If there are a lot of clouds covering the Moon, just draw what you see that night.

3. Don't forget, when it's a new Moon, you won't see anything, so just draw a dark sky.

crescent

first quarter

gibbous

full Moon

Quiz

1 What do we call the phase of the Moon when we can't see it at all?
2 How many times have humans landed on the Moon?
3 How many times a month does the Moon circle the Earth?
4 What do we call the Moon's vast dry plains?
5 Is the Moon made of cheese?
6 What is an "earthquake" on the Moon called?

DID SOMEBODY SAY CHEESE?

Answers
1 New Moon. 2 Six. 3 Once.
4 Seas (because people once thought they were water).
5 No (only in fairy tales!). 6 Moonquake.

SOLAR SYSTEM

Our Earth is one of nine planets that travel around the Sun. Along with many moons, lumps of rock and comets, the Sun and its orbiting planets make up the solar system (solar means "to do with the Sun"). Everything in the solar system is connected to the Sun, at its centre, by an invisible force called gravity.

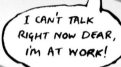

> I CAN'T TALK RIGHT NOW DEAR, I'M AT WORK!

Quiz

1 Which is the second biggest planet?

2 How many planets have people walked on?

3 Which planet is smaller than our Moon?

4 What colour does Earth look from space?

5 Which two planets do not have moons?

6 Which planet was named after the Roman god of the sea?

Mercury

Venus

Earth

Answers
1 Saturn. 2 One – Earth. 3 Pluto.
4 Blue. 5 Mercury and Venus.
6 Neptune.

Factfile

- The largest planet, Jupiter, is big enough to hold over 1,300 Earths.
- The planet closest to the Sun, Mercury, travels around the Sun six times in one of our Earth years.
- The four giant outer planets – Jupiter, Saturn, Uranus and Neptune – are made of gas around a rocky core.
- Pluto is over a hundred times further away from the Sun than Mercury is.
- There are thousands of miniature planets, called asteroids, in the space between Mars and Jupiter.

Pluto

Neptune

Uranus

Saturn

Jupiter

Mars

GOOD JOB
I REMEMBERED
MY SPACE MAP!

Plasticine planets

1. You can mould plasticine around small round objects – beads, marbles, ping-pong balls – to make planets. Follow the colours on these pages for each one.
2. Mould a big yellow Sun around a larger ball.
3. Then put the planets in order on a black paper space background.

SUN

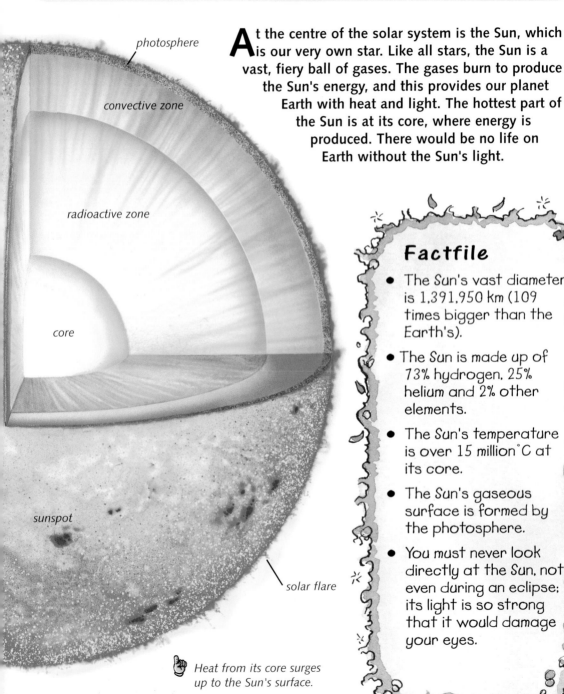

photosphere

convective zone

radioactive zone

core

sunspot

solar flare

At the centre of the solar system is the Sun, which is our very own star. Like all stars, the Sun is a vast, fiery ball of gases. The gases burn to produce the Sun's energy, and this provides our planet Earth with heat and light. The hottest part of the Sun is at its core, where energy is produced. There would be no life on Earth without the Sun's light.

Factfile

- The Sun's vast diameter is 1,391,950 km (109 times bigger than the Earth's).

- The Sun is made up of 73% hydrogen, 25% helium and 2% other elements.

- The Sun's temperature is over 15 million°C at its core.

- The Sun's gaseous surface is formed by the photosphere.

- You must never look directly at the Sun, not even during an eclipse; its light is so strong that it would damage your eyes.

Heat from its core surges up to the Sun's surface.

Sometimes the Moon is in the exact position to block out the Sun for a few minutes. This is called a solar eclipse.

Make a sundial clock

1. Push the blunt end of a pencil into plasticine and stand it on a piece of white card.

2. Starting in the morning on a sunny day, use a ruler and pen to mark where the shadow of the pencil falls every hour. Write the time next to the line (10 o'clock, 11 o'clock, and so on).

3. On the next sunny day, you can use your sundial clock to tell the time (remember, the card must remain in exactly the same spot).

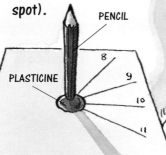

PENCIL

PLASTICINE

8
9
10
11

Quiz

1 How many Earths would it take to make a ball as large as the Sun – more than a hundred, a thousand or a million?

2 What are small, dark patches on the Sun called?

3 The Earth is not always exactly the same distance from the Sun – true or false?

4 How long does it take for the Sun's rays to reach Earth – eight seconds, eight minutes or eight hours?

5 Is the Sun the biggest star?

6 How long does it take for the Earth to travel around the Sun?

Answers
1 More than a million.
2 Sunspots. 3 True. 4 Eight minutes. 5 No. 6 A year.

AHH ... THIS IS THE LIFE!

THE SUN IS HOTTEST ON THE PLANETS NEAREST TO IT, AND COOLER ON THOSE FURTHER AWAY!

DAYS AND SEASONS

The Earth is constantly spinning, like a top. At any one time, about half of the planet is facing the Sun, and this half is in daylight. As that half turns away from the Sun because of the Earth's spin, it gets dark and has night-time.

PHEW!

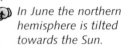
In June the northern hemisphere is tilted towards the Sun.

Factfile

- In the tropics, the hottest parts of the Earth near the Equator, it is warm all year round.

- Many trees drop their leaves in the autumn; this helps them survive the cold, dark winter.

- Twice during the year day and night are the same length of 12 hours each; the two equinoxes are on 21 March and 23 September.

- In the northern hemisphere, the longest day is around 21 June, and the shortest day around 21 December.

In September the northern and southern hemispheres receive equal amounts of Sun.

The Earth is slightly tilted on its axis, and this tilt causes the seasons. When the northern half of the planet is tilted towards the Sun, it is summer there. At the same time it is winter in the southern hemisphere, because that lower half is tilted away from the Sun's warmth.

The Earth spins right round once every 24 hours.

In June the northern half of the Earth is tilted towards the Sun. In December it is the exact opposite.

In March the northern and southern hemispheres receive equal amounts of Sun.

In December the southern hemisphere is tilted towards the Sun.

Quiz

1 How many times does the Earth spin round in a year?

2 When it's summer in Europe, what season is it in Australia?

3 Which season comes after winter?

4 What is the southern half of the Earth called?

5 What is the northern tropic called?

6 When it's spring in London, what season is it in New York?

Answers
1 365 times. 2 Winter 3 Spring.
4 Southern hemisphere.
5 Tropic of Cancer 6 spring.

STOP THE WORLD, I WANT TO GET OFF

Day and night

1. For this activity, you need a globe of the Earth. If you haven't got one, use a plastic football and pretend. Your globe/ball is the Earth, and for the Sun you will need a torch.

2. In a darkened room, shine the torch at your globe. The side facing the torch (or Sun) is lit up, so there it is day. On the dark side of the globe it is night.

3. If you slowly spin the globe round, you will see how daylight moves around the Earth.

STARS

The night sky is full of stars. In fact, the day sky is full of them too, but the light from our local star, the Sun, blots them out. Each of the stars is a huge ball of gas that gives off vast amounts of light and heat. There are millions upon millions of stars in the universe. Some of them are so far away from Earth that it has taken millions of years for their light to reach us. When a star has used up all its energy, it stops shining and dies.

A nebula is a glowing cloud of dust and gas.

BEWARE BLACK HOLES!

TUG TUG

A star burns from a nuclear reaction inside it

A red supergiant is an enormous star, 500 times the diameter of our Sun.

Quiz

1   Are some stars smaller than our Sun?

2   Some stars that we see in the night sky may no longer exist – true or false?

3   Have humans ever travelled to another star?

4   What is another name for the North Star?

5   Will our star, the Sun, ever die?

6   What are binary stars?

Factfile

Some stars are brighter than others; but a dim star that is close to our solar system can appear brighter than a more distant, brighter star.

Astronomers measure in light years, which is the distance travelled by light in a year (equivalent to 9.46 million million km).

- The nearest star to our solar system is Proxima Centauri, which is 4.2 light years away.

The brightest star in the night sky is Sirius, the dog-star.

Star mural

1. Let the stars twinkle on your wall. Cut out star shapes from shiny sweet wrappers. Use gold and silver foil for very bright stars. Stick the stars on a large sheet of black paper.

2. Brush some PVA glue onto the background and sprinkle on some glitter for a sparkling Milky Way. Shake off any unwanted glitter.

3. Then stick your star mural up on the wall with multi-purpose tac.

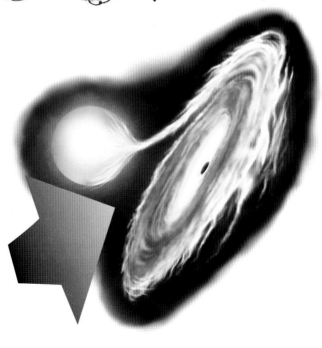

Some stars explode and produce a supernova.

The material left collapses in on itself. The gravity around that spot is so strong that not even light can escape, which is why it is called a black hole.

GALAXIES

Stars cluster together in groups called galaxies. These clusters have different shapes. Some are round, ball shapes, while others are completely irregular. All galaxies are spinning in space, and the shape of a galaxy depends on how fast it spins.

The Sun is just one of millions of stars in our galaxy, which is called the Milky Way. Ours is a spiral galaxy, and it got its name because from Earth it looks like a creamy band of stars across the sky.

Our star, the Sun, is on a spiral arm of the Milky Way galaxy.

This spiral galaxy is very similar in appearance to our own Milky Way.

Quiz

1 The word "galaxy" comes from an Ancient Greek term meaning what?

2 What is the constellation that looks like fishes called?

3 How long does it take light to travel right across the Milky Way?

4 The constellation of Libra is not an animal or a person, but what?

5 Is the Sun at the centre of the Milky Way galaxy?

6 How many constellations make up the signs of the zodiac?

Answers
1 Milk. 2 Pisces. 3 160,000 years.
4 Scales, or Balance
5 No. 6 Twelve.

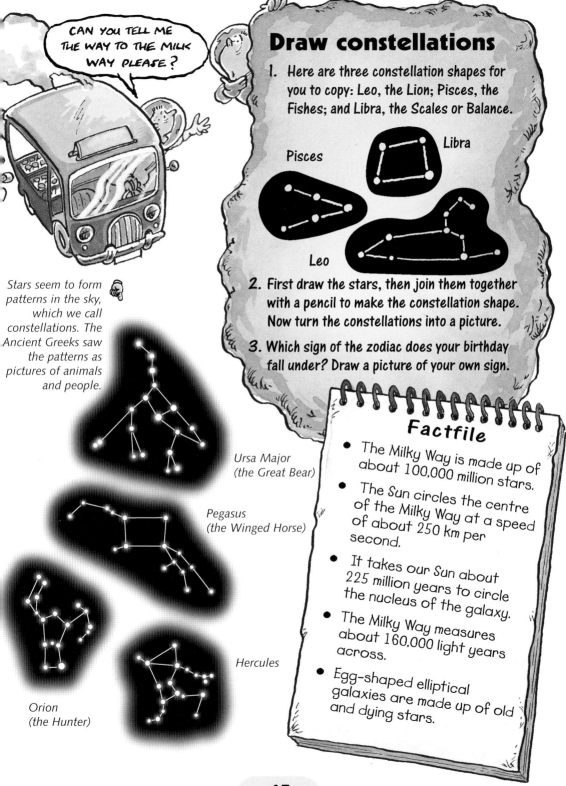

CAN YOU TELL ME THE WAY TO THE MILK WAY PLEASE?

Draw constellations

1. Here are three constellation shapes for you to copy: Leo, the Lion; Pisces, the Fishes; and Libra, the Scales or Balance.

Pisces

Libra

Leo

2. First draw the stars, then join them together with a pencil to make the constellation shape. Now turn the constellations into a picture.

3. Which sign of the zodiac does your birthday fall under? Draw a picture of your own sign.

Stars seem to form patterns in the sky, which we call constellations. The Ancient Greeks saw the patterns as pictures of animals and people.

Ursa Major
(the Great Bear)

Pegasus
(the Winged Horse)

Hercules

Orion
(the Hunter)

Factfile

- The Milky Way is made up of about 100,000 million stars.

- The Sun circles the centre of the Milky Way at a speed of about 250 km per second.

- It takes our Sun about 225 million years to circle the nucleus of the galaxy.

- The Milky Way measures about 160,000 light years across.

- Egg-shaped elliptical galaxies are made up of old and dying stars.

UNIVERSE

The Universe is the whole of space. It is the biggest thing there is, including all the stars, galaxies and the empty parts of space between them. We can only see a very small part of the Universe, even with the most powerful telescope.

Most scientists think that the Universe began with a Big Bang, about 15,000 million years ago. Since then it has been growing bigger and bigger in all directions, creating more and more space. The Universe is still expanding today.

The Big Bang was a massive explosion that created the Universe.

Millions of years later, gases clustered into clouds.

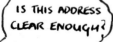

IS THIS ADDRESS CLEAR ENOUGH?

Josie Bloggs
8 Acacia Avenue
Surbiton, Surrey
England
Europe
Earth
Solar System
Milky Way
Universe

The clouds clumped together to form galaxies.

We can see millions of stars in the night sky, but these are still just a tiny part of the Universe.

Expanding the Universe

1. Paint white, squiggly galaxies on a big blue or black balloon.

2. Let the paint dry, and then slowly blow up the balloon. As air fills it, you will see the galaxies moving apart, just as they are really doing in the Universe. If you stand in front of a mirror, you can see this more clearly.

MERCURY AND VENUS

Mercury

Venus

Mercury is the closest of the solar system's nine planets to the Sun. It is a small, rocky planet, which looks a bit like our Moon and is not much larger. The side of Mercury facing the Sun gets blisteringly hot – more than 420°C – because it is so close. The other side, however, is freezing cold – about -180°C.

The next planet out from the Sun, Venus, is slightly smaller than Earth. It has a thick atmosphere of carbon dioxide gas, which traps the Sun's heat and makes it even hotter than on Mercury.

Factfile

- Diameter: Mercury 4,878 km; Venus 12,104 km.

- Distance from the Sun: Mercury 58 million km; Venus 108 million km.

- Spin time in Earth days: Mercury 59; Venus 243.

- Orbit time around the Sun in Earth days: Mercury 88; Venus 225.

- Moons: neither planet has any moons.

- Venus' atmosphere pushes down with a pressure more than 90 times stronger than air pressure on Earth.

Mercury's surface has many small craters, like our Moon.

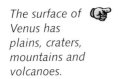

The surface of Venus has plains, craters, mountains and volcanoes.

MY VERY EARLY MORNING JAM SANDWICH USUALLY NAUSEATES PEOPLE. THAT'S HOW I REMEMBER THE ORDER OF THE PLANETS, MERCURY, VENUS, EARTH ...

COOKING OIL

WATER

FLOUR

Crater baking

1. To bake your own Mercurial craters, mix 250 g plain flour with 125 g salt and two spoonfuls of cooking oil. Mix in a little water until you have a non-sticky mixture.

2. Mould the dough to make a Mercuryscape, and use a fork and spoon to create craters.

3. Ask an adult for help. Line a baking sheet with foil and bake Mercury at the bottom of the oven for about 30 minutes at 180° centigrade or gas mark four. When it has cooled, put it on a cardboard base and paint the craters grey and black.

MARS

Mars is sometimes called the red planet, because its rocks and soil are a reddish colour. This is caused by iron oxide, the chemical name for rust. There is no running water on Mars, but dried-up river beds show that Mars did have water millions of years ago. The Viking spacecraft landed on the planet in 1976, and in 1997 the Pathfinder spacecraft sent the Sojourner rover vehicle to study the rocks on Mars and photograph them.

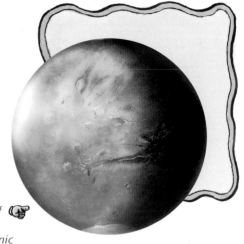

The surface of 👉 Mars shows signs of volcanic activity.

👉 The six-wheeled, remote-controlled rover named Sojourner was specially designed to move about on Mars.

Factfile

- Diameter: 6,787 km.
- Distance from the Sun: 228 million km.
- Spin time in Earth days: one (24 hours and 37 minutes).
- Orbit time around the Sun in Earth days: 687.
- Moons: two; the irregular-shaped Deimos is 12 km across and is the smallest moon in the solar system; Mars' other moon, Phobos, is a bit larger.
- Atmosphere: 95% carbon dioxide and 3% nitrogen, with traces of oxygen, argon, carbon monoxide and water.

Quiz

1 Mars was named after the Roman god of what?

2 How long did it take *Pathfinder* to fly to Mars from Earth – seven weeks, seven months or seven years?

3 Mars has two polar icecaps – true or false?

4 How many planets are there between Mars and Pluto?

5 Which has a longer day, Mars or Earth?

6 Which US spacecraft first flew close to Mars in 1965?

Answers

1 War. 2 Seven months. 3 True. 4 Four. 5 Mars. 6 Mariner.

Olympus Mons is the largest of Mars' four giant volcanoes. It is 600 km across at the base and 27 km high.

Marbled Mars

1. To make marbled Mars paper, put blobs of orange, red and brown oil paint on a plate.

2. With the help of an adult, mix a few drops of white spirit into it with a knife, to make the paint runny.

3. Use a bowl of water that is at least as big as your piece of paper. Plop the paint off the knife into the water and swirl it round gently. Alternatively, you can put drops of marbling ink straight into the water.

4. Place your paper on top of the floating colours for 30 seconds. Then lift it off, turn it over and hold it flat to stop the paint running.

5. When the paper is dry, you can use it as Martian gift-wrap.

THE HIGHEST POINT ON EARTH IS ONLY A THIRD AS HIGH AS OLYMPUS MONS

GRRRR

JUPITER

The largest planet in the solar system lies beyond a band of mini-planets called the asteroid belt. Jupiter is a gas giant, made mainly of hydrogen around a rock-iron core. The planet is so big that its core alone weighs about 15 times more than planet Earth.

It has large cloud features that swirl around its surface, as well as a system of rings that were only discovered in 1979.

Jupiter's four biggest moons are sometimes called the Galilean moons, because in 1610 the famous Italian astronomer Galileo discovered them.

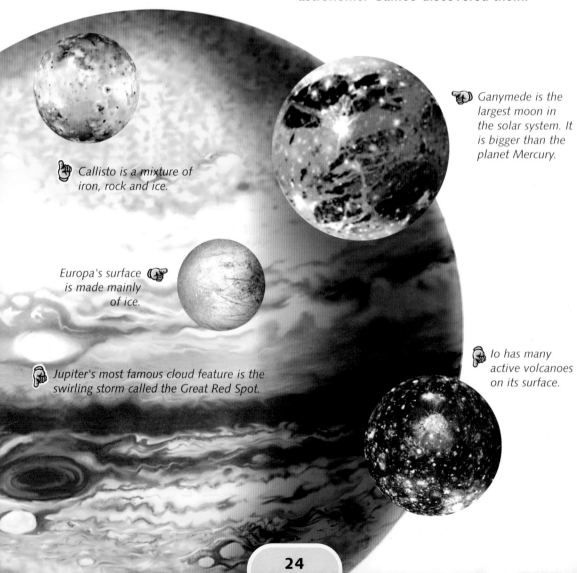

Ganymede is the largest moon in the solar system. It is bigger than the planet Mercury.

Callisto is a mixture of iron, rock and ice.

Europa's surface is made mainly of ice.

Jupiter's most famous cloud feature is the swirling storm called the Great Red Spot.

Io has many active volcanoes on its surface.

Factfile

- Diameter: 142,796 km.
- Distance from the Sun: 778 million km.
- Spin time in Earth hours: ten.
- Jupiter's rings have three parts: an inner halo, a bright central ring, and an outer thin ring which extends out to 214,000 km.
- Moons: 16, including the four Galilean moons.
- Orbit time around the Sun in Earth years: 11.9.

I'M JUPITER, KING OF THE ROMAN GODS; THIS PLANET WAS NAMED AFTER ME.

Zoom off to Jupiter

1. Everyone who plays this game is on the way to Jupiter, but who will get there first?

2. Copy the board on a large piece of card. Starting at square one, move your counter according to the number you throw on a dice.

3. Every time you land on a square with the bottom of a rocket, zoom to the top. When you land on the tail of a comet, you must slide right down to the head. When you land on a lost-in-space square, you miss a turn. You might be lucky and meet a friendly alien who'll show you a short cut to Jupiter.

SATURN

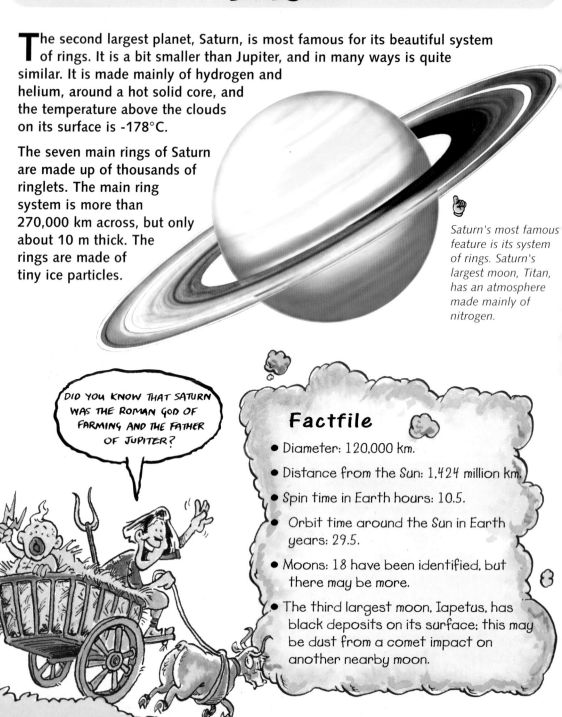

The second largest planet, Saturn, is most famous for its beautiful system of rings. It is a bit smaller than Jupiter, and in many ways is quite similar. It is made mainly of hydrogen and helium, around a hot solid core, and the temperature above the clouds on its surface is -178°C.

The seven main rings of Saturn are made up of thousands of ringlets. The main ring system is more than 270,000 km across, but only about 10 m thick. The rings are made of tiny ice particles.

Saturn's most famous feature is its system of rings. Saturn's largest moon, Titan, has an atmosphere made mainly of nitrogen.

DID YOU KNOW THAT SATURN WAS THE ROMAN GOD OF FARMING AND THE FATHER OF JUPITER?

Factfile

- Diameter: 120,000 km.
- Distance from the Sun: 1,424 million km.
- Spin time in Earth hours: 10.5.
- Orbit time around the Sun in Earth years: 29.5.
- Moons: 18 have been identified, but there may be more.
- The third largest moon, Iapetus, has black deposits on its surface; this may be dust from a comet impact on another nearby moon.

Quiz

1. How many complete orbits of the Sun does Earth make while Saturn makes one?

2. Titan is the only moon in the solar system with a real atmosphere – true or false?

3. How many times does Saturn spin around in an Earth day?

4. What is the basic colour of Saturn – blue, green or yellow?

5. Is Saturn visible from Earth without a telescope?

6. Which day of the week comes from the god Saturn?

Galileo first observed Saturn's rings in 1610, but their true nature was discovered by the Dutch astronomer Christiaan Huygens 49 years later.

Hang up Saturn

1. Screw some newspaper into a ball (about 15 cm in diameter) and secure it with masking tape.

2. Tear newspaper into small strips. Mix some PVA glue and water into a paste and dip the strips in. Cover the ball evenly.

3. Now cover the ball with white paper strips and leave the model to dry. Then paint it yellow.

4. Draw a 17 cm wide circle on card. Then draw a 20 cm circle around it. Cut out the inner circle, then cut around the outer line and paint rings of colour on your card circle.

5. Attach the ring to Saturn with card tabs. Stick the tabs to the ring, fold them and tape them to the planet, leaving a small gap all around.

6. Tape nylon thread to Saturn and hang it from the ceiling.

BALL OF NEWSPAPER

WHITE PAPER STRIPS

PAPER RING

CARD TABS

URANUS, NEPTUNE AND PLUTO

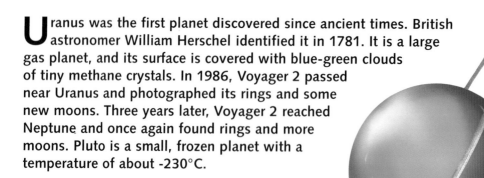

Uranus was the first planet discovered since ancient times. British astronomer William Herschel identified it in 1781. It is a large gas planet, and its surface is covered with blue-green clouds of tiny methane crystals. In 1986, Voyager 2 passed near Uranus and photographed its rings and some new moons. Three years later, Voyager 2 reached Neptune and once again found rings and more moons. Pluto is a small, frozen planet with a temperature of about -230°C.

Neptune was discovered in 1846 by the German astronomer Johann Gottfried Galle.

Uranus' rings are almost vertical, because the planet has turned over onto its side.

Pluto is the smallest planet in our Solar System, and the furthest from the Sun.

Factfile

- Diameter: Uranus 51,118 km; Neptune 49,532 km; Pluto 2,320 km.

- Distance from the Sun: Uranus 2,866 million km; Neptune 4,488 million km; Pluto 5,906 million km.

- Spin time in Earth hours: Uranus 17; Neptune 16; Pluto 154 (over six days).

- Orbit time around the Sun in Earth years: Uranus 84; Neptune 165; Pluto 248.

- Moons: Uranus 15; Neptune eight; Pluto one

- Pluto's single moon, Charon, is about half its size; its surface is covered in ice.

Planets and gods

Which planet is named after which god?
Follow the jumbled lines with your finger to find out.

God of the heavens

God of the sea

Pluto

Neptune

Uranus

God of the underworld

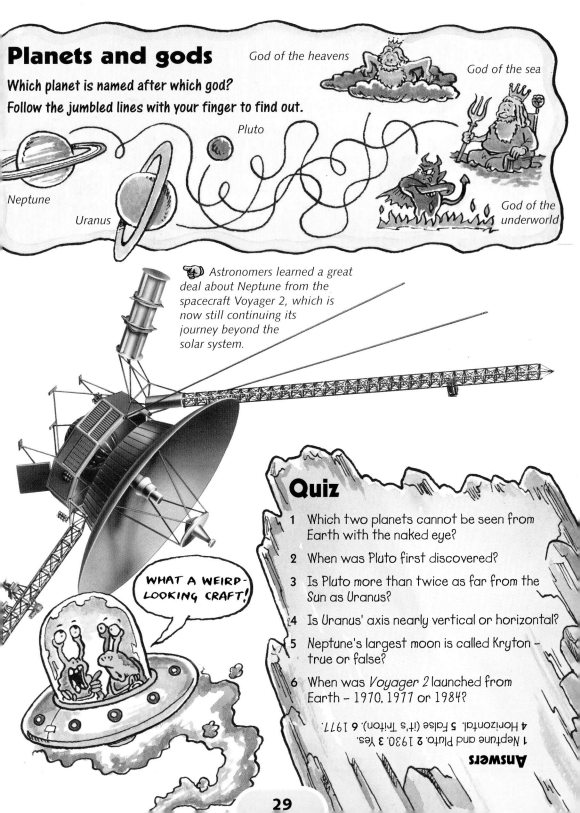

Astronomers learned a great deal about Neptune from the spacecraft *Voyager 2*, which is now still continuing its journey beyond the solar system.

WHAT A WEIRD-LOOKING CRAFT!

Quiz

1 Which two planets cannot be seen from Earth with the naked eye?

2 When was Pluto first discovered?

3 Is Pluto more than twice as far from the Sun as Uranus?

4 Is Uranus' axis nearly vertical or horizontal?

5 Neptune's largest moon is called Kryton – true or false?

6 When was *Voyager 2* launched from Earth – 1970, 1977 or 1984?

Answers

1 Neptune and Pluto. 2 1930. 3 Yes.
4 Horizontal. 5 False (it's Triton). 6 1977.

COMETS AND METEORS

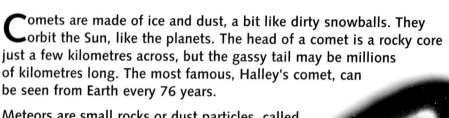

Comets are made of ice and dust, a bit like dirty snowballs. They orbit the Sun, like the planets. The head of a comet is a rocky core just a few kilometres across, but the gassy tail may be millions of kilometres long. The most famous, Halley's comet, can be seen from Earth every 76 years.

Meteors are small rocks or dust particles, called meteoroids out in space, that burn up as they enter the Earth's atmosphere. The burning makes a streak of light with a bright trail in the night sky.

A comet's tail always points away from the Sun.

Meteoroids become meteorites if they land on Earth's surface.

EDWAR

Factfile

- Comets usually have long, oval orbits, which take them a long way from the Sun.

- The largest meteorite ever found on Earth fell on Namibia in 1920; it was 2.7 m long and 2.4 m wide.

- The biggest comets are up to 180 km across.

- The largest crater made by a meteorite is Meteor Crater in Arizona, USA; the hole is 1,275 m across and 175 m deep; it was made by a meteor crashing into Earth about 50,000 years ago.

Pilot a spaceship

1. Join your spaceship at the bottom left of the picture.

2. Then, with your finger, try to pilot the spaceship on a safe flight path past all the meteoroids and comets, till you reach the other side.

HOME

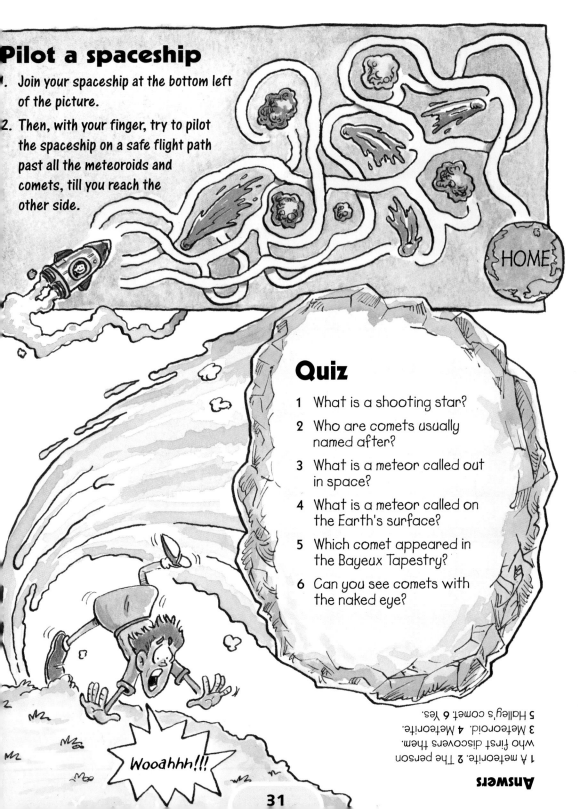

Wooahhh!!!

Quiz

1. What is a shooting star?

2. Who are comets usually named after?

3. What is a meteor called out in space?

4. What is a meteor called on the Earth's surface?

5. Which comet appeared in the Bayeux Tapestry?

6. Can you see comets with the naked eye?

TRAVELLING IN SPACE

The first person to travel in space was a Russian, Yuri Gagarin, who circled the Earth once in 1961. A few weeks later the Americans sent their first astronaut into space – for just 15 minutes. Eight years later space travel had developed so much that a man was standing on the surface of the Moon. Since then astronauts have learned to live in space for longer periods and have conducted many useful experiments. There are even plans to send astronauts to Mars in the future.

FRANK, I THINK YOU'VE FORGOTTEN SOMETHIN

An astronaut can move freely through space on a special Manned Manoeuvring Unit, or MMU, which is guided by small jets.

Factfile

- In space there is so little gravity that everything floats, including astronauts and their food.

- The first living thing to travel in space was a dog called Laika, in 1957.

- There were five more successful Moon landings after *Apollo 11* in 1969.

- The first woman in space was Russian Valentina Tereshkova in 1963.

- On the last Apollo mission to the Moon, astronauts spent 76 hours on the lunar surface.

Make a moonscape

1. Mix four cups of plain flour and one cup of salt in a bowl. Add some yellow food colouring to a mug of water. Stir in as much water as needed, a little at a time, and knead it into a non-sticky mixture.

2. Shape the dough into a lunar surface with mountains and craters. You could even make some astronauts' footprints.

3. To make a lunar module, cover an eggbox cup with silver foil and stick a toothpaste lid on top. Shorten four bendy straws and glue them to the cup. Each leg is held with plasticine in a toothpaste-lid foot.

Neil Armstrong was the first human to set foot on the Moon when he left his lunar module, called Eagle.

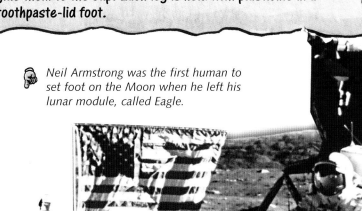

Quiz

1 What was the four-wheeled vehicle that astronauts took to the Moon called?

2 Who was the first American in space?

3 What is a Russian astronaut called?

4 Did all the astronauts who landed on the Moon get back to Earth safely?

5 Is there air inside a spacecraft?

6 Is there air on the Moon?

Answers
1 Lunar Rover. 2 Alan Shepard.
3 Cosmonaut 4 Yes.
5 Yes. 6 No.

ROCKETS

Spacecraft, astronauts and satellites are launched into space by huge rockets. These work in the same way as firework rockets, burning fuel to force hot gases out at the back and so push the rocket forwards. Powerful space rockets burn enormous amounts of fuel very quickly, and most have two or three stages, which are really separate rockets stacked on top of each other. All this energy is needed to escape the pull of Earth's gravity.

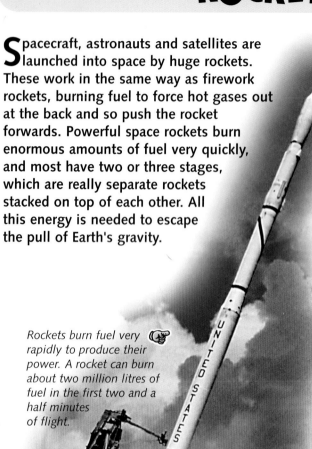

ahhh!!!

Rockets burn fuel very *rapidly to produce their power. A rocket can burn about two million litres of fuel in the first two and a half minutes of flight.*

Factfile

- Spacecraft need a speed of over 40,000 km/h (20 times faster than a Concorde plane) to escape Earth's gravity and get out into space.

- Gunpowder firework rockets were invented in Ancient China.

- The first space rocket was launched in Massachusetts, USA, in 1926, but it only reached a height of 12.5 m!

- Saturn V was 111 m tall and blasted off with the power equivalent to 160 jumbo jet engines.

Quiz

1. Rockets carry their own supply of oxygen, so that their fuel will burn in space – true or false?
2. At which space centre are American rockets launched?
3. In which country are Russian rockets launched?
4. What does NASA stand for?
5. In which American city was mission control for the Moon landings?
6. Ariane rockets are launched by ESA; what does ESA stand for?

Answers

1 True. 2 Kennedy Space Center 3 Kazakhstan.
4 National Aeronautics and Space Administration.
5 Houston, Texas. 6 European Space Agency.

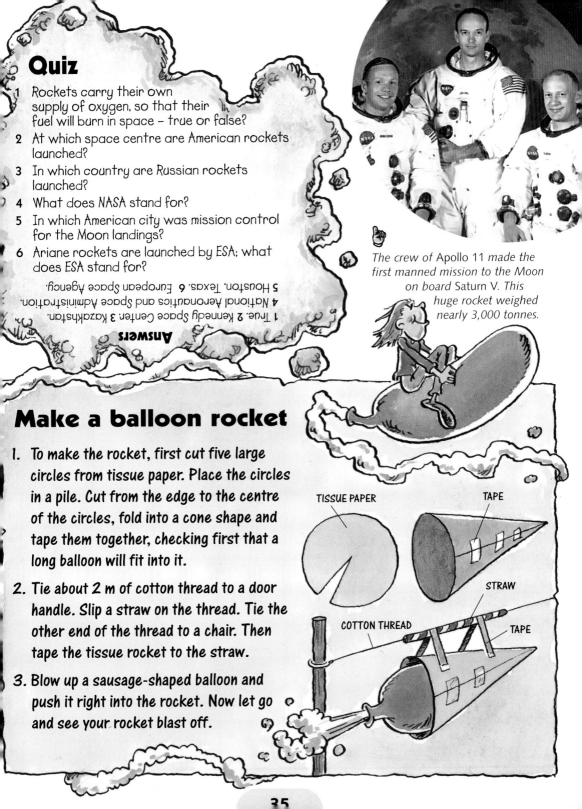

The crew of Apollo 11 made the first manned mission to the Moon on board Saturn V. This huge rocket weighed nearly 3,000 tonnes.

Make a balloon rocket

1. To make the rocket, first cut five large circles from tissue paper. Place the circles in a pile. Cut from the edge to the centre of the circles, fold into a cone shape and tape them together, checking first that a long balloon will fit into it.

2. Tie about 2 m of cotton thread to a door handle. Slip a straw on the thread. Tie the other end of the thread to a chair. Then tape the tissue rocket to the straw.

3. Blow up a sausage-shaped balloon and push it right into the rocket. Now let go and see your rocket blast off.

TISSUE PAPER

TAPE

STRAW

COTTON THREAD

TAPE

SHUTTLE

During the 1960s and 1970s space travel was extremely expensive because rockets and spacecraft were only ever used once. Then scientists invented the space shuttle, a reusable craft that can fly into space and land on Earth again many times. The American space shuttle Columbia was first launched in 1981, and since then shuttles have been used to take satellites into space, as well as taking astronauts to and from space stations.

Then the empty fuel tank separates.

After launch, the two booster rockets fall away from the shuttle.

The space shuttle is launched on the back of a huge fuel tank and two extra booster rockets.

I'VE BOOKED TO GO ON THE FIRST SPACE SHUTTLE SERVICE FOR PAYING PASSENGERS.

Factfile

- An American space shuttle can carry up to seven astronauts, plus a cargo of satellites.

- The landing runway at Kennedy Space Center is 4,572 m long.

- In 1986 shuttle *Challenger* exploded after take-off and all seven astronauts were killed.

- A shuttle's main fuel tank is 47 m long.

- Space shuttles are taken to the launch pad on a crawler-transporter that moves on eight sets of caterpillar tracks at a top speed of 1.6 km/h.

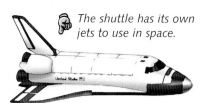

The shuttle has its own jets to use in space.

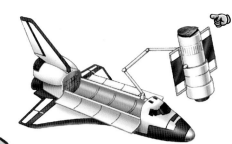

The shuttle is used to take satellites into space. It can also take astronauts to help fix satellites if they go wrong in orbit.

Quiz

1 How long is a US shuttle – 27 m, 37 m or 47 m?

2 Are the shuttle's booster rockets re-used?

3 What was the name of the fifth US shuttle, launched in 1992?

4 How many crew does the crawler-transporter have – 6, 16 or 26?

5 In which US state is Kennedy Space Center?

6 What is the shuttle's cargo hold called?

Answers
1 37 m. 2 Yes. 3 *Endeavour*. 4 26. 5 Florida. 6 Payload bay.

The shuttle glows red-hot when it re-enters the Earth's atmosphere.

The shuttle lands like a giant glider on a long runway.

Make a space shuttle

1. Put a large plastic bottle on a piece of white card. Draw one shuttle wing, as shown. Fold the card in half and cut along the pencil line. Tape the wings to the bottle.

2. Cut out a tailpiece and tape it on the shuttle. Tape two yoghurt-pot engines at each side. Make a nose cone from a cardboard circle. Cut a segment out of the circle, form it into a cone and fit it around the bottle top.

3. Paint the shuttle white with acrylic paint. (Poster paint mixed with a few drops of washing-up liquid will also stick to plastic.)

4. When the white paint is dry, decorate your shuttle with stickers and silver foil. For a fiery exhaust, stick strips of red, yellow and pink paper inside the engines.

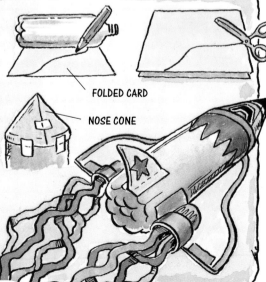

FOLDED CARD

NOSE CONE

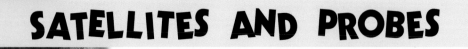

SATELLITES AND PROBES

Hundreds of manmade space satellites are orbiting the Earth and sending back information all the time. Some send phone calls or television pictures around the world, while others help weather forecasters or help fix a position on Earth for sailors or even mountaineers.

Space probes have explored the planets, many of their moons, comets and other parts of space. They carry cameras and other equipment to give scientists close-up information that they simply could not gain from Earth.

Phone messages and TV pictures are sent up to telecommunications satellites, which bounce the information back to another part of the world.

Factfile

- Some satellites will stay in orbit around the Earth for hundreds or thousands of years; they will become space junk, along with old bits of rockets and other manmade material.

- In 1970, a year after *Apollo 11* landed on the Moon, an unmanned Luna craft brought Moon rock back to Earth, and a Lunokhod probe crawled over the lunar surface.

- The *International Violet Explorer* satellite was launched in 1978 and was expected to send back information for three years; to scientists' amazement, it went on working for 18 years.

HOUSTON, WE HAVE A PROBLEM!!

In 1976 two Viking probes landed on Mars, photographed the landscape and measured wind, temperature and other features.

Communications breakdown

1. The radio waves are all jumbled up. Can you work out which communications satellite is beaming information to which dish aerial?

2. Follow the lines from each satellite with your finger, until you reach the right dish.

A.

B.

C.

1.

2.

3.

TELESCOPES

Astronomers use very powerful telescopes to see as far as possible out into the Universe. The telescopes have a mirror or lens to collect the light from an object. Big telescopes are protected inside domed buildings called observatories. The shape of the dome allows the telescope to rotate completely, giving astronomers a view of the entire night sky. In 1990 the Hubble space telescope was launched by a shuttle, and this has given even better views from space.

The Hubble space telescope was designed to see objects seven times further away than Earth-based telescopes.

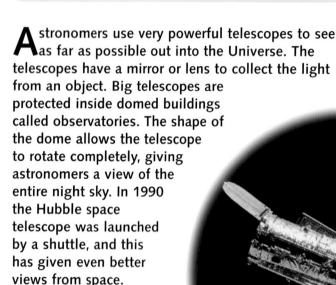

Factfile

- Radio telescopes pick up and send radio signals. The world's largest radio telescope at Arecibo, in Puerto Rico has a 305 m dish.

- In December 1993, astronauts on shuttle *Endeavour* spent over 35 hours servicing and correcting faults on the Hubble space telescope – in space!

- The two Keck telescopes on Mauna Kea mountain, Hawaii, are the largest in the world. Each telescope has a 10 m mirror.

- The Very Large Telescope on top of a mountain in northern Chile is actually a group of four telescopes that work together.

WOW, THERE'S SOMEONE LOOKING BACK AT ME!

Star-gazing

1. It's fun to star-gaze with friends and family. On a clear, dark night you can usually see hundreds of stars with the naked eye. If you use a pair of binoculars, you should be able to see thousands of stars – and much more clearly.

2. One way to identify stars and constellations is to use a planisphere, which is a star map that you can turn round and set to a specific time.

3. If you want to find out more or start using a telescope, you could join your local astronomical society.

WOW, THERE'S SOMEONE LOOKING BACK AT ME!!

Quiz

1. Which famous Italian scientist helped develop the telescope in 1609?

2. What was the first name of the US astronomer who gave his name to the space telescope?

3. Who designed the Royal Greenwich Observatory (in 1675)?

4. What does VLT stand for?

5. What are the two large panels on the sides of the space telescope designed to catch?

6. What is a scientist who studies space and the stars called?

The best observatories are on mountain tops, well away from the bright lights of cities.

Answers

1 Galileo. 2 Edwin (Hubble). 3 Sir Christopher Wren. 4 Very Large Telescope. 5 Solar energy. 6 An astronomer.

SPACE STATIONS

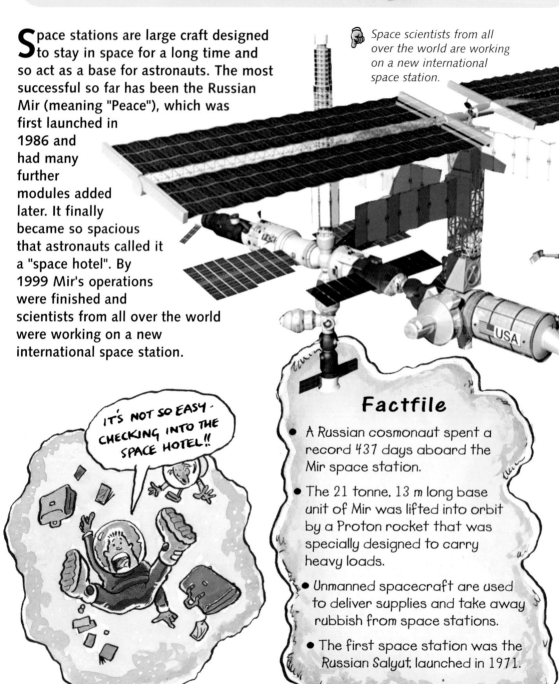

Space stations are large craft designed to stay in space for a long time and so act as a base for astronauts. The most successful so far has been the Russian Mir (meaning "Peace"), which was first launched in 1986 and had many further modules added later. It finally became so spacious that astronauts called it a "space hotel". By 1999 Mir's operations were finished and scientists from all over the world were working on a new international space station.

Space scientists from all over the world are working on a new international space station.

IT'S NOT SO EASY - CHECKING INTO THE SPACE HOTEL!!

Factfile

- A Russian cosmonaut spent a record 437 days aboard the Mir space station.

- The 21 tonne, 13 m long base unit of Mir was lifted into orbit by a Proton rocket that was specially designed to carry heavy loads.

- Unmanned spacecraft are used to deliver supplies and take away rubbish from space stations.

- The first space station was the Russian Salyut, launched in 1971.

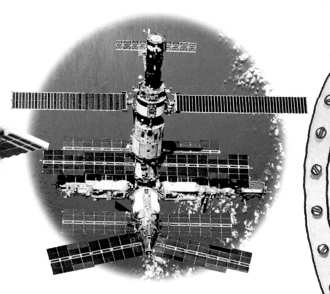

☞ The Russian space station Mir started off as a small project, but grew as further modules were added and astronauts from other nations visited it.

Junk station

1. Mark a large piece of cardboard into three sections and stand it up. The panels are your control room. Fix various sizes of cardboard boxes and cartons along the top, bottom and sides with tape, and then paint them.

2. For the instrument panels use old metal scraps, nuts, bolts and lids; any old parts from broken radios, bikes, clocks and other machines could be useful too. Attach them to the boxes with strong glue.

3. For essential space equipment cover dishes, tubes and yoghurt pots with silver foil. Put up charts, graphs and space-age designs. Then get in touch with ground control!

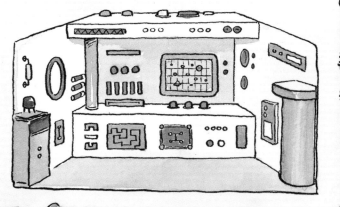

LIFE IN SPACE?

Are there other forms of life in the Universe, apart from human beings, animals and plants on Earth? We don't know, but many scientists believe this is very likely. Some people claim to have seen strange spacecraft approaching Earth, but most of these "unidentified flying objects" have been explained or have proved to be hoaxes. Others claim to have seen aliens – beings from another world. Unmanned probes have found no signs of life on other planets in our Solar System. But Martian rocks found on Earth show that there may once have been microscopic forms of life on Mars.

Supposed alien spacecraft are sometimes called "flying saucers". They might look more like this one.

In many science fiction books and films, aliens are shown as unfriendly. But perhaps they would want to be friends with us.

44

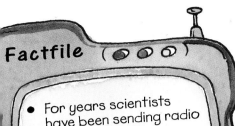

- For years scientists have been sending radio signals into space, hoping for a reply; they haven't had one yet.

- Astronomers have discovered planets orbiting stars outside our Solar System; perhaps there is life on one of those planets?

- There are millions of stars in our galaxy, and millions of galaxies in the Universe: isn't it likely that life exists on more than one small planet?

Playdough aliens

1. Get out the playdough – the more colours you can find the better– and make some alien friends.

2. There are no limits in space. Odd shaped creatures, long thin sausage aliens and round heads without bodies might all live in a galaxy far, far away.

3. You can add pipe-cleaners, buttons and other bits and pieces for that Extra-Terrestrial touch.

Quiz

1 What does UFO stand for?

2 What are the inhabitants of Earth called?

3 What does ET stand for?

4 Who made the Star Wars films?

5 What is the name of the doctor who time-travels in the Tardis?

6 Does alien life exist?

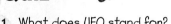

Answers

1 Unidentified Flying Object
2 Earthlings. 3 Extra-Terrestrial.
4 George Lucas. 5 Dr Who.
6 Give your own answer – we don't know!

IT MUST BE SOME SORT OF WEIRD RITUAL, THEY WATCH IT ALL THE TIME!

INTO THE FUTURE

What will happen to the Universe in the future? Most scientists believe that it will go on expanding, until – many millions of years from now – the galaxies start to fall back towards the centre of the Universe and come together in a big crunch. Our star, the Sun, won't last that long, but will burn out in about 5,000 million years time.

In the near future, humans may find ways to visit other planets and even stars. Scientists are already working on a new mission, to send astronauts to Mars.

Mars is a very cold and windy planet. A Martian base for humans will need protective buildings with their own air supply.

Factfile

- The furthest humans have travelled is to the Moon. Mars is over 200 times further away.

- The fastest speed at which humans have ever travelled is around 40,000 km/h; light travels 27,000 times faster than this!

- If humans ever found a way to travel at the speed of light, which scientists think is the fastest speed possible in the Universe, it would still take over four years to reach the next nearest star to the Sun.

- Some scientists think that a future Big Crunch might be followed by another Big Bang – all in millions and millions of years time.

WELL, IT SAYS IT'S HOT IN THE BROCHURE

In future, faster space planes may take over from shuttles, so that humans can visit other planets.

Foil space city

1. Collect plastic packaging, cardboard tubes, egg cartons, plastic bottles, yoghurt pots, cans, lids, tops and foil dishes.

2. You need the base of a large cardboard box to build your space city on. Study your collection first and decide on a layout for the city before glueing everything down.

3. Cover all the items with foil. Plastic bottles cut in half make domes for Earthlings to live in. Tubes and cans make a network of passages connecting buildings and towers. Satellite dishes can be made from lids and foil.

4. Stick everything to the cardboard base, then paint the base white. Wait for it to dry before moving into foil city.

Index